1003

Salt & Pepper

Shakers *with values*

Larry Carey & Sylvia Tompkins

Schiffer Publishing Ltd

77 Lower Valley Road, Atglen, PA 19310

Printed in China

ISBN: 0-7643-0112-8

Book Design by Audrey L. Whiteside

Library of Congress Cataloging-in-Publication Data

Carey, Larry.
    1003 salt & pepper shakers / Larry Carey & Sylvia Tompkins.
        p. cm.
    Includes bibliographcial references and index.
    ISBN 0-7643-0112-8 (pbk.)
    1. Character salt and pepper shakers--Collectors and collecting--Catalogs.   I. Tompkins, Sylvia. II. Title.
NK8640.C372   1997
730'.075--dc20   96-29169
                                                    CIP

Published by Schiffer Publishing, Ltd.
77 Lower Valley Road
Atglen, PA 19310
Phone: (610) 593-1777
Fax: (610) 593-2002
Please write for a free catalog.
This book may be purchased from the publisher.
Please include $2.95 for shipping.
Try your bookstore first.
We are interested in hearing from authors
with book ideas on related subjects.

ACKNOWLEDGMENTS

We greatly appreciate the encouragement and assistance of fellow collectors and especially the following contributors to this book:

Gaye Adsett
Michelle Bady
Trish Claar
Frances Clements
Nigel Dalley
Marilyn DiPrima
Pat Disney
Joyce & Bill Fisher
Jeanne Fouts
Bob Gentile
Shirley Gimondo
Marty Grossman
Lorraine Haywood
Wendy R. Johnston
Gary Levenson
Eric Lodge
Phil Mays
Clara & Hubert McHugh
Jean Moon
Muriel O'Connor
Rich O'Donnell
Sandy Piggott
Judy & Jeff Posner
Joyce & Fred Roerig
Joanne Rose
Diana & Larry Sanderson
Barbara & Mike Schwarz
Marcia Smith
Irene Thornburg
'Tiques Auction
The Wengels
Ruth & Ken Wittlief
Betsy Zalewski

Our special thanks to Marty Grossman and Judy and Jeff Posner whose insistence led to our decision to address the subject of character salt & pepper shakers, and whose assistance has been invaluable. Friends, we couldn't have done it without you.

TABLE OF CONTENTS

INTRODUCTION

Included in this book are basically three categories of characters: comic strip and cartoon; TV, movie, and other entertainment forms; and mascots or symbols, such as Smokey the Bear or the Loch Ness monster. This extremely popular area of salt and pepper shakers appeals to a wide range of collecting interests and crosses many boundaries of collectibles.

A substantial part of this book is devoted to the salt and pepper shakers representing characters created by Walt Disney and continued by the Disney Studio after his death. The major characters, notably Mickey Mouse and his gang, developed and changed over the years, but the transition was so gradual it was hardly noticeable at the time.

Licensing information is provided as marked on the sets. Some of the early sets, primarily those produced in Germany prior to World War II, were licensed but not marked. Unmarked sets are subject to personal interpretation, influenced by the eye of the beholder.

Values are based upon our experience and input from contributors. They are intended as a guide only and will vary depending on condition, geographical area, knowledge of the seller or buyer, and to some extent, sheer luck.

Plans for our next book include literary characters, which we ran out of room for this time; famous people; and childrens literature (kiddie lit/children's world) such as nursery rhymes and fables.

The Novelty Salt & Pepper Shakers club

The 1500 members of the Novelty Salt & Pepper Shakers Club have discovered the enjoyment and benefit to be derived from joining with others who share a love for our hobby. Each year the Club convention is held in a different part of the country to afford the opportunity for attendance to as many members as possible. Our four annual newsletters provide information on shaker identification and history, as well as the chance to buy, sell, and trade. For more information about this Club, contact the authors.

DISNEY

Mickey Mouse's first appearance was on November 18, 1928, in "Steamboat Willie," the first animated movie with synchronized sound. He was Walt Disney's favorite and his greatest star. This movie also was the first for Minnie Mouse. 1930 saw the arrival of Pluto, initially as Minnie's dog; this soon changed into the famous friendship of Mickey and Pluto. Goofy first appeared in 1932 in "Mickey's Revue." Donald Duck came into being in 1934 in "The Wise Little Hen" as a bit player, and proceeded to steal the show. He is one of the world's most popular stars. Daisy Duck's first role came in 1937 in "Don Donald."

Mickey and Minnie Mouse

Mickeys. 3.25". Japan. 1940s. $200+.

Mickeys. 3". Japan. 1930s. $200+.

Mickey. 3". Japan. 1940s. If a pair, $200+.

Mickeys. 3.5". Japan. 1940s. $200+.

Mickeys. 3.5". Japan. 1940s. $200+.

Mickeys. 3.5". Japan. 1930s. $200+.

Mickeys. 4". Japan. 1980s. Probably licensed, label with Japanese writing 90 yen. $100-125.

Mickeys. 4.5". Japan. 1960s. Stamped Dan Brechner WD-31. © Walt Disney Productions. Also shown in original wrapper. $125-150.

Mickeys 3". USA. 1950s. Leeds China. © Walt Disney Productions. All of the gold trimmed Leeds Disney shakers apparently have three holes. $75-85.

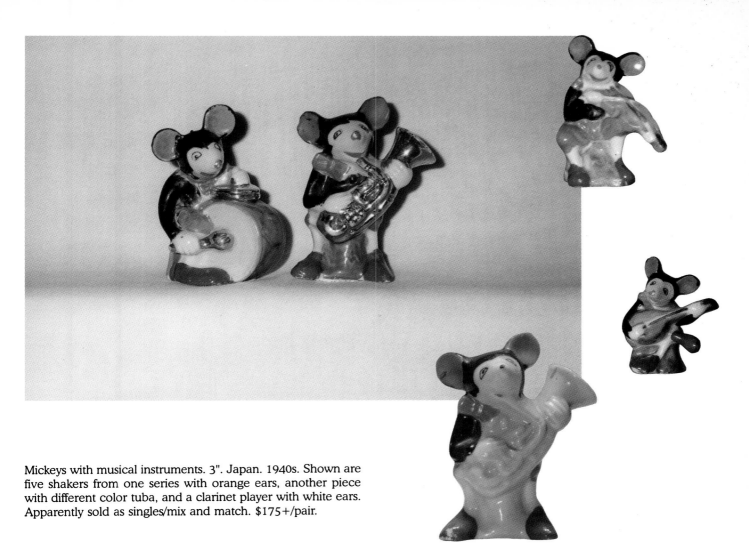

Mickeys with musical instruments. 3". Japan. 1940s. Shown are five shakers from one series with orange ears, another piece with different color tuba, and a clarinet player with white ears. Apparently sold as singles/mix and match. $175+/pair.

Mickeys and Minnies. 3.25". Germany. 1930s. $400+.

Mickey and Minnie. 2.5". Germany. 1930s. $500+.

Mickeys. 2.75". Germany. 1930s. Both five holes, large and small size. $500+.

Mickeys. 2.25". Germany. 1940s. Note: this set has a thicker neck and ankles than copy on the right, also is slightly taller. $250+.

Mickeys. 2". Germany. 1990s. 1 and 5 holes, ceramic has a chalky appearance and feel, believed to be a copy of set on the left. Offered for sale by German dealer for $250 in mid-1990s. $75-100.

Mickey condiments. 3.75". Germany. 1930s. Note difference in eyes and tails. Rare, $500+.

Mickey condiment with open salt and pepper. 3.5". Germany. 1930s. $500+.

Mickey open salt and pepper. 1.75". Germany. 1930s. Allemagne stamp (imported into France). $300+.

Mickey condiment. 3.25". Germany. 1930s. $500+.

Mickey condiment. 3.75". Germany. 1930s. Mickey S&P same as those used in the cat condiments. $500+.

"Murz der Kater und die Mickymäuschen" (Murz the Tomcat and the Mickey Mouses) condiment. 3". Germany. 1930s. A Disney comic book was published in Germany in 1935 with this title and we believe the condiment is based on this comic. $500+.

Mickey chefs. 4". Taiwan. 1990. © The Walt Disney Company. Issued by Hoan Ltd. $20-25.

Mickey Merry Christmas. 3.5". Japan. 1980s. © Disney. $45-50.

Mickeys in cottages, front and back views. 3". Japan. 1960s. © Walt Disney Productions. $30-35.

Mickey chefs. 2.75". Japan. 1970s. Left set, © Walt Disney Productions. Right set, © Disney. $35-40.

Mickeys on glass shakers, plastic tops. 3". Probably USA. 1930s. © Walt E. Disney. $150+.

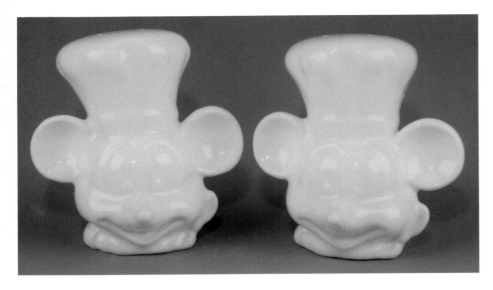

3-D Mickey chefs. 5". USA. 1980s. Treasure Craft. $30-35.

Mickey Executive Dining Room. 3.5". Mexico. 1990s. Porcelain. Treasure Craft. © WDP. $25-30.

Mickey chefs. 4.75". 1980s. T.C. USA. © Walt Disney Productions. $30-35.

Gourmet Mickey. 4". Probably Japan. 1980s. © The Walt Disney Company. Distributed by Walt Disney World, Lake Buena Vista, Florida. $25-30.

Gourmet Mickey Seasoning Collection. 5". Treasure Craft. USA. © Walt Disney Company. Foil label "Ouverture en 1992 Euro Disney" (Opening in 1992). Issue price $21. Current value $50-60.

Mickey in chair. 3.5". Korea. 1990s. © The Walt Disney Company. Applause Inc. $20-25.

Mickey in car. 3.25". Korea. 1990s. © The Walt Disney Company. Applause Inc. $20-25.

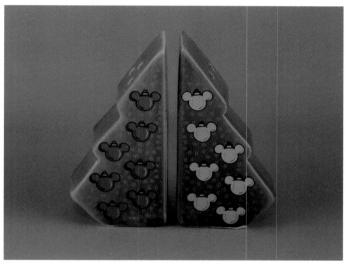

Mickey in a sleigh. 4.25". Korea. 1990. © The Walt Disney Company. Applause, Inc. $50-60.

Mickey heads on Christmas tree. 3.5" Taiwan. 1990s. © Walt Disney Company. Applause Inc. $20-25.

Sorcerer Mickey. 3.5". Malaysia. 1990s. © Disney. $25-30.

Mickey on ski jump. 4.25". Indonesia. 1990s. © Disney. Enesco. $18-20.

Mickey and jukebox. 4". China. 1990s. © Disney. Enesco. $18-20.

Mickey playing piano. 4". Indonesia. 1990s. © Disney. Enesco. $18-20.

Mickey in canoe. 4". China. 1990s. © Disney. Enesco. $18-20.

Mickey with pot of gold. 3.5". China. 1990s. © Disney. Enesco. $20-25.

Mickey's hands. 4.25". USA. 1995. © Disney. Pfaltzgraff. $25-30.

Mickey's glove and pants. 2.25". China. 1990s. © Disney. $25-30.

Mickey and Goofy. 3". Probably Japan. 1950s. $250+.

Minnies and Mickeys. 1.5". Germany. 1980s. © Disney. Reutter Porzellan. $35-40.

Mickey and Minnie. 4". Japan. 1950s. $150+.

Mickey and Minnie. 3". Probably Japan. 1940s. $200+.

Mickey and Minnie. 2.5". Germany. 1940s. $300+.

Mickey and Minnie condiment. 3.75". Japan. 1930s. $500+.

Mickey and Minnie on wooden bench. 4.25". Japan. 1960s. Dan Brechner. © Walt Disney Productions. $125-150.

Mickey and Minnie on squealer bases. 5.25". Japan. 1960s. Dan Brechner WD-52. © Walt Disney Productions. $125-150.

Mickey and Minnie. 3". USA. 1950s. Leeds China. © Walt Disney Productions. If excellent condition, $40-45.

Mickey and Minnie on glass. 2.75". Japan. 1980s. © Walt Disney Productions. Label: A Gift of Glass from Walt Disney World. Issue price $2.75. Current value $12-15.

Mickey and Minnie on glass. 5". Japan. 1980s. © Walt Disney Productions. She says "salt" and he says "pepper." $40-50.

Mickey and Minnie. 3.25". USA. 1950s. © Walt Disney Productions. Leeds China. Made of china-like material rather than ceramic, possibly a prototype, probably sold unpainted. $65-75.

Mickey and Minnie. 2.75". 1990s. © The Walt Disney Company. Applause Inc. $20-25.

Mickey and Minnie. 3". Country unknown. 1990s. New England Collectors Society. $50-55.

Mickey and Minnie. 3.75". Malaysia. 1990s. © Disney. $25-30.

Mickey and Minnie. 5.25". Mexico. 1990s. © Disney. Treasure Craft. $25-30.

Mickey and Minnie. 4.25". Taiwan. 1995. © Disney in Canada. $25-30.

Mickey and Minnie. 3.75". Taiwan. 1995. © Disney in Canada. $20-25.

Mickey and Minnie dancing. 4". Korea. 1990s. © The Walt Disney Company. Applause, Inc. $45-50.

Mickey and Minnie Christmas. 3.25". China. 1990s. © Disney. Enesco. $20-25.

Mickey and Minnie. 3". COR, Germany. 1980s. © Walt Disney Company. $90-100.

Mickey and Minnie. 3". China. 1990s. © Disney. Enesco. $20-25.

Mickey and Minnie. 3". Japan. 1980s. © Walt Disney Productions. $75-85.

Mickey and Minnie. Christmas set. 3". Country unknown. 1990s. New England Collectors Society. $50-55.

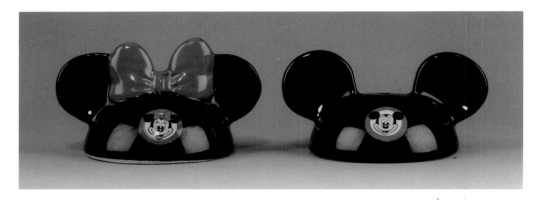

Mickey & Minnie hats. 1.75". Korea. 1991. © The Walt Disney Company. Applause Inc. $20-25.

Minnie and vanity. 4". Indonesia. 1990s. © Disney. Enesco. $18-20.

Minnie with gifts. 5". Indonesia. 1990s. © Disney. Enesco. $18-20.

Morty and Ferdie, Mickey's nephews. 2.75". Country unknown. 1990s. New England Collectors Society. $50-55.

Minnie's bow and shoe. 2". China. 1990s. © Disney. $25-30.

Goofy

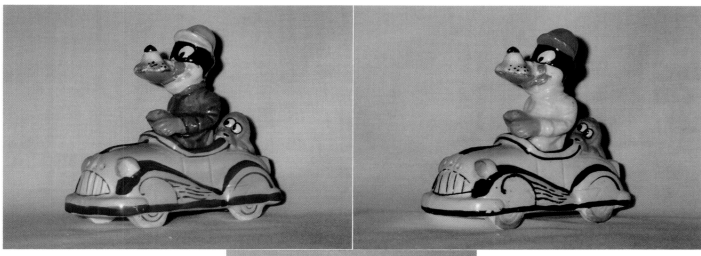

Goofy driving a car. 4". Japan. 1940s. $400+.

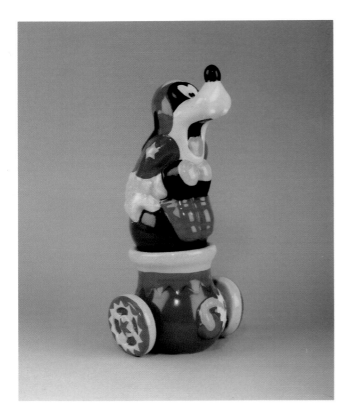

Goofy on cannon. 6.5". China. 1990s. © Disney. Enesco. $18-20.

Goofy driving car. 4.5". Malaysia. 1990s. © Disney. $25-30.

Goofy and cake. 3.5". Country unknown. 1990s. New England Collectors Society. $50-55.

Goofy and tepee. 3.5". Indonesia. 1990s. © Disney. Enesco. $18-20.

Pluto

Pluto, first and second sets, 3.25". Third set, 3.75". Japan. 1960s. Note different angle of cups. $90-

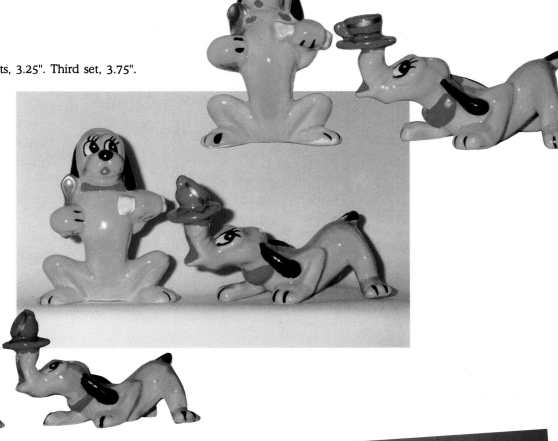

Pluto. 3.25". USA. 1950s. © W.D.P. Incised. Gold trim, $65-75. Red trim, $30-35.

Pluto. 4.25". Japan. 1960s. Fuzzy. $15-20.

Butch and Pluto. 3.5". Country unknown. 1990s. New England Collectors Society. $50-55.

Mickey and Pluto. 3.75". Malaysia. 1990s. © Disney. $25-30.

Pluto and his house. 2.75". China. 1990s. © Disney. $25-30.

Pluto and his house. 3". Korea. 1990s. © The Walt Disney Company. Applause Inc. $20-25.

Pluto and his house. 3.5". Indonesia. 1990s. © Disney. Enesco. $18-20.

Donald Duck and Family

Donald, single. 4". Japan. 1960s. "I've lost my mate." $25-30.

Donald on a raft. 3.75". Japan. 1950s. $200+.

Right: Donalds. 2.75". Japan. 1960s. $20-25.

Left: Donalds. 3.5". Japan. 1940s. $45-50.

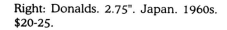

Right: Donald driving a speed boat. 3.25". Japan. 1950s. $150+.

Above: Donalds. 3". Japan. 1940s. $35-40.

Donalds. 4". USA. 1950s. Donald Duck © Walt Disney. Leeds China. $90-100.

Above: Donald and nephews. 6". Japan. 1960s. $75-85.

Donald and Daisy. Japan. 1960s. $65-75.

Donalds. 3.25". USA. 1950s. © Walt Disney Productions. Leeds China. $50-60.

Donalds. 3.25". USA. 1950s. © Walt Disney. Leeds China $75-85.

Donald and barbecue grill. 4.25". Indonesia. 1990s. © Disney. Enesco. $18-20.

Huey, Dewey, and Louie. 2.75". Country unknown. 1990s. New England Collectors Society. $50-55.

Donald and the salt mine cart. 4.25". 1990s. © The Walt Disney Company. Applause Inc. $20-25.

Two nephews. 2.75". USA. 1950s. © Walt Disney. Chalkware. In good condition, $90-100.

One of the nephews. 2.25". 1950s. Seven Pottery. "Help, I need a mate." Unpriced.

Two nephews. 4". Japan. 1950s. $200+.

Donald and nephews condiment. 4.75". Japan. 1950s. Mustard top missing. If complete, $500+.

Donald and nephews condiment. 5". Japan. 1960s. Note: Spoon is tongue. $200+.

Daisy. 3.75". Japan. 1950s. $20-25.

Daisy and shopping bag. 3.25". Korea. 1990s. © The Walt Disney Company. Applause Inc. $20-25.

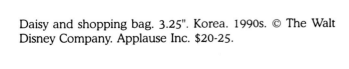

Donald and Daisy. 3.25". Japan. 1950s. $35-40.

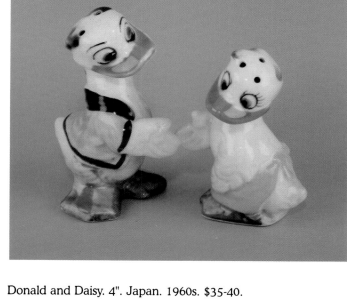

Donald and Daisy. 4". Japan. 1960s. $35-40.

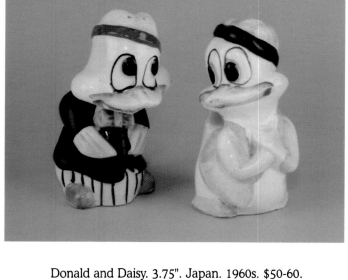

Donald and Daisy. 3.75". Japan. 1960s. $50-60.

Daisy and Donald. 3.25". Japan. 1960s. $40-50.

Donald and Daisy. 3.5". Country unknown. 1990s. New England Collectors Society. $50-55.

Donald and Daisy. 4". Japan. 1950s. $45-50.

Daisy and Donald. 4". Japan. 1950s. $45-50.

Donalds and Ludwig von Drakes. 4.5". Japan. © 1961 Walt Disney Productions. Dan Brechner WD 32 and WD 33. $125-150.

Donald and Ludwig von Drake. 5.25". Japan. © 1961 Walt Disney Productions. Dan Brechner. $125-150.

Scrooge and the money bags. 3". Country unknown. 1990s. New England Collectors Society. $50-55.

Scrooge. 4". Japan. 1950s. $150+.

Alice in Wonderland

Alice in Wonderland. 5". USA. 1950s. Incised name. © Walt Disney Productions. Regal China. $400+.

Alice and the caterpillar. 4.5". Japan. 1960s. Name incised on front of base. $100-110.

Mad Hatter and Mouse. 3.5". Taiwan. 1990s. Applause Inc. $12-15.

White Rabbits. Left set, 4". Right set, 3.25". Japan. 1950s. $65-75.

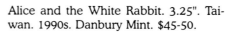

White rabbit. 3". Probably USA. 1950s. No marks. Single $40-45.

Alice and the White Rabbit. 3.25". Taiwan. 1990s. Danbury Mint. $45-50.

White Rabbit condiment. 5". Japan. 1960s. $85-95.

Alice and the Mad Hatter, 3.5". Country unknown. 1990s. New England Collectors Society. $50-55.

Tweedle Dee and Tweedle Dum. 3.5". USA. 1960s. $150+.

Tweedle Dee and Tweedle Dum. 4.25".
Taiwan. 1992. Fitz and Floyd. $35-40.

Tweedle Dee and Tweedle Dum. 3.25".
Taiwan. 1990s. Danbury Mint. $45-50.

Tweedle Dee and Tweedle Dum. 4.5". USA. Regal China. 1950s.
Walt Disney Prod. Extremely rare, $700+.

Bongo and Lulubelle from "Fun and Fancy Free." Left set, 4.75". Right set, 4.25". Center is a figurine licensed to Sidney Pottery, Australia. Sets Japan. 1960s. $50-60.

Bongo and Lulubelle. 2.25". Nikoniko China, Japan. 1950s. $90-100.

Chip an' Dale from "Chips Ahoy" and other movies. 3.5". USA. 1960s. Brad Shaw in raised letters. $75-85.

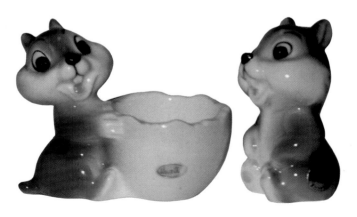

Chip an' Dale. 2.5". Probably Japan. 1960s. Foil label Walt Disney Productions. $250+.

Chip an' Dale. 3". Country unknown. 1990s. New England Collectors Society. $50-55.

Cinderella and her coach. 2.5". USA. 1950s. $75-85.

Cinderella and the Fairy God-mother. 3.25". Taiwan. 1990s. Danbury Mint. $45-50.

Cinderella and her slipper. 4.25". China. 1990s. © Disney. $25-30.

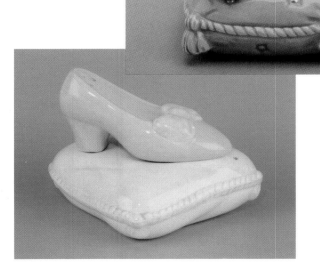

Cinderella's slipper. 3". Sri Lanka. 1990s. Fitz & Floyd. $25-30.

Cinderella's slipper. 2.75". China. 1990s. Applause Inc. $12-15.

Gus & Jaq Mice. 2.75". Weetman Giftware, England. 1960s. $250+.

Bambis. 3.25". Japan. 1960s. $25-35.

Bambi and Faline. 3.75". Japan. 1960s. Napco/Giftcraft. $25-35.

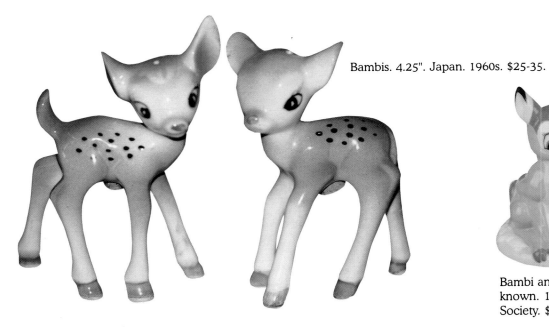

Bambis. 4.25". Japan. 1960s. $25-35.

Bambi and Thumper. 2.75". Country unknown. 1990s. New England Collectors Society. $50-55.

Thumpers. Eyes closed, 2.25". Eyes open, 3". Germany. 1950s. Label: Walt Disney, Thumper Character, WDP FFM © Goebel, full bee stamp, (R), and © Goebel crown stamp. $150-175.

Thumpers. 2.5". Germany. Designed in 1950s. Red and yellow produced to 1980s. Brown and green produced 1960s. Goebel set number DIS 40, later sets usually sold in white baskets. Red and yellow, $50-60. Brown and green, $90-100.

Thumpers. 3.75". Germany. 1970s. Goebel DIS 40. $50-60.

Thumper. 3.25". Germany. 1950s. Goebel. Licensed. $125-150 pair.

Thumpers. 3". England. 1960s. $150-175.

Thumpers. 3.5". England. 1960s. $90-100.

Thumpers. 3.25". USA. 1950s. © Walt Disney Productions. Leeds China. Made of china-like material rather than ceramic, possibly a prototype, probably sold unpainted. $65-75.

Thumpers. 3.25". USA. 1950s. © Walt Disney Productions. Leeds China. $40-45.

Thumpers. 3.25". Japan. 1960s. Kreiss. $35-40.

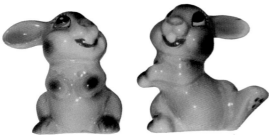

Thumpers. 2.5". Japan. 1950s. $40-50.

Thumpers. 3.5". Probably Japan. 1960s. $35-40.

Flower. 3". Goebel, Germany. 1950s. Note left set has no eyelashes, right set does. $175+.

Flower. 2.5". Japan. 1950s. PY. $75-85.

Friend Owl and Flower condiment. 5". Japan. 1960s. $125-150.

Flower. 3.25". Japan. 1960s. $25-30.

Flower. 3". Japan. 1950s. $40-50.

Dumbo

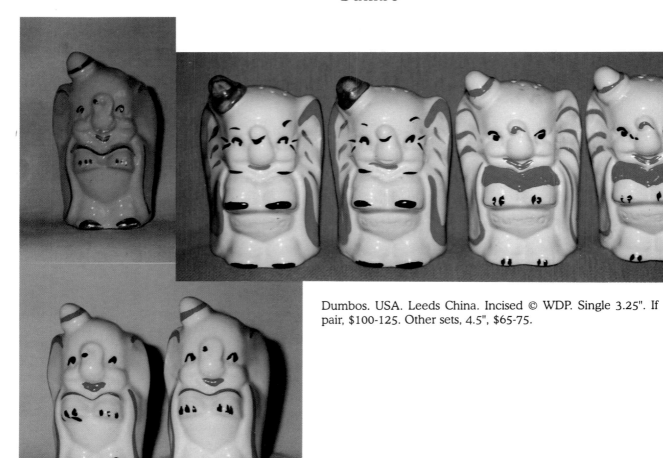

Dumbos. USA. Leeds China. Incised © WDP. Single 3.25". If pair, $100-125. Other sets, 4.5", $65-75.

Dumbos. 2.75". Japan. 1960s. $45-50.

Dumbos. 3.25". USA. American Pottery. Incised Walt Disney on back. $45-50.

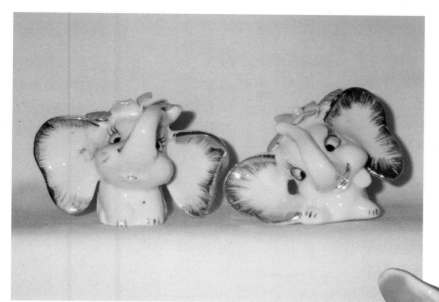

Dumbos. 2.5". Japan. 1950s. $45-50.

Dumbos. 3". Japan. 1960s. $45-50.

Dumbos. 2". Probably Japan. 1960s. $35-40.

Dumbos. 2". 1950s. A Quality Product, Japan label. $65-75.

Dumbo and Mrs. Jumbo, Dumbo's mother. 2.75". Japan. 1960s. $85-100.

Dumbo and Timothy Mouse. 2.5". Japan. 1960s. $45-50.

Timothy. 3". Japan. 1950s. $65-75.

The firemen. 4.25". Japan. 1960s. $45-50.

The crows: Fat Crow, Dandy Crow, Glasses Crow, Preacher Crow, and Straw Hat Crow.

Preacher and Dandy. 3.5". Japan. 1940s. Enesco Imports. $75-85.

A series of the crows in varying poses. 4". Japan. 1950s. $65-75.

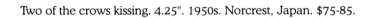

Two of the crows kissing. 4.25". 1950s. Norcrest, Japan. $75-85.

Two of the crows. 3.25". 1950s. PY Japan. $75-85.

Pink elephants. In the most famous scene of the film, Dumbo hallucinates a big group of dancing, trumpeting pink elephants.

Three sets. 2.25". Japan. 1960s. $45-50.

S&Ps hang on body. 4". Japan. 1960s. $50-60.

Salt and pepper heads rest on sugar and creamer bodies. 5". Japan. 1960s. $65-75.

S&P, oil and vinegar hang on body. 5.5". Japan. 1960s. $65-75.

Elmer Elephant from a Silly Symphony. 3". Japan. 1940s. Composition material marked sample. $125-135.

Donald Duck & Elmer Elephant. 3". Japan. 1940s. $125-135.

Ferdinand the Bull. 2.5," 2.75". Japan. 1950s. Black sets, $65-75. Other sets, $75-85.

Fantasía

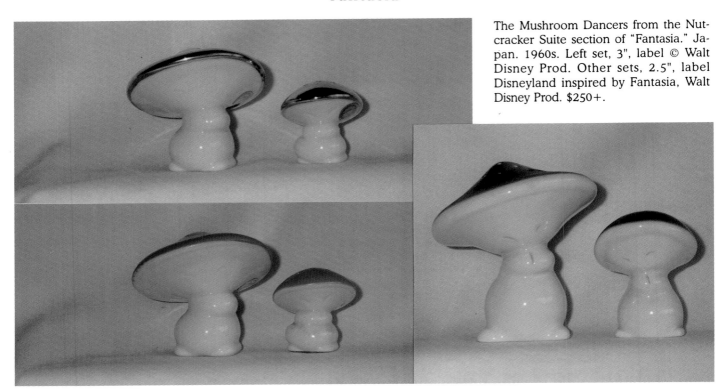

The Mushroom Dancers from the Nutcracker Suite section of "Fantasia." Japan. 1960s. Left set, 3", label © Walt Disney Prod. Other sets, 2.5", label Disneyland inspired by Fantasia, Walt Disney Prod. $250+.

Fantasia. 3". Designed by Walt Disney, copyright 1940, Vernon Kilns. Made in USA. Autumn Ballet pattern. If a pair, $175+.

Hop Low, one of the mushroom dancers. First set, 3.25", Disney copyright 1941 Vernon Kilns USA. Second set, 3.5". Label © Disney Fantasia, American Pottery Co. Los Angeles, also produced by Evan K. Shaw. Third set, 4.5", Japan. $125-150.

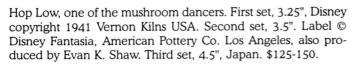

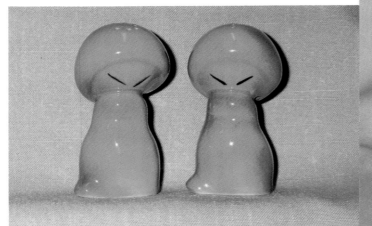

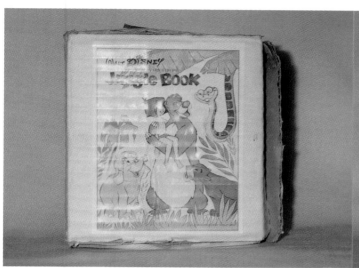

Mowgli & Baby Elephant from "The Jungle Book." 4.75". Japan. © Walt Disney Prod. MCMLXIV. Enesco. $150-175.

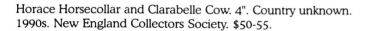

Jose Carioca from "The Three Caballeros." 3". Japan. 1960s. © Kreiss. $35-40.

Horace Horsecollar and Clarabelle Cow. 4". Country unknown. 1990s. New England Collectors Society. $50-55.

Lady and The Tramp

This is the best known series of the dogs. 2"-3.75".
Japan. 1960s. $90-100.

Lady & The Tramp

Dachsie & Pedro

Trusty & Jock

Boris & Toughy

This is part of another series of the dogs. 3.5".
Japan. 1960s. $60-70.

Lady and The Tramp

Boris

Toughy

Jock in different colors

Lady and Tramp. 3.5". Country unknown. 1990s. New England
Collectors Society. $50-55.

Another series where two-of-a-kind are a pair.

Lady. 3". Japan. 1960s. Enesco Imports. $60-70.

Tramp. 4.25". Japan. 1960s. $40-50.

Dachsie. 2.25". Japan. 1960s. $40-50.

Dachsie. 2". Japan. 1960s. $40-50.

Tramp. 4.25". Japan. 1960s. $40-50.

Trusty. 3.5". Japan. 1960s. $40-50.

Jock. 3.25". 1960s. PY Ucago, Japan. Issue price 69 cents. Current value $60-70.

Lady and The Tramp. 3". Probably Japan. 1970s. From Tony's Town Square Restaurant in Disney World. $75-85.

Trusty & Jock. 3". 1960s. PY Japan. $75-85.

Pedro & Jock. 3". 1960s. Enesco, Japan. Probably two singles. $40-50.

Tramp. 3.25" h, 9.5" l. Japan. 1960s. One-piece set. $75-85.

Tony & Joe, restaurateur and chef from "Lady and the Tramp." 4.25". Japan. 1960s. Possibly Napco. $75-85.

Si and Am. 3.5". Paper label, Japan. 1950s. Six poses shown.
$100-125.

The Lion King. 4". USA. 1990s. © Disney. Treasure Craft. $25-30.

Ariel, The Little Mermaid, and Flounder. 5.25". China. 1990s. © Disney. $25-30.

Main Street Policemen from Disneyland. 3.75". Japan. 1960s. © Walt Disney Productions, blue trapezoid mark on bottom. $100-125.

Genie and the Lamp from "Aladdin." 5.75". USA. 1990s. © Disney. Treasure Craft. $35-40.

Abner, the Country Mouse & Monty, the City Mouse, from "The Country Cousin." 2.75". Japan. 1950s. $40-50.

Cereal Sisters, Miss Corn & Miss Oats. 2.5". Japan. © 1981 Walt Disney Prod. Featured at the Kraft Kabaret at Epcot Center, Florida, $65-75.

Peter Pan

Tinker Bell. 2". Japan. 1960s. Green trapezoid mark Disneyland, © Walt Disney Productions. $25-30.

Peter Pan and Wendy. 3.25". Taiwan. 1990s. Danbury Mint. $45-50.

Tinker Bell. 2.5". Japan. 1960s. © Walt Disney Productions. $25-30.

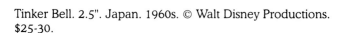

Tinker Bell and castle. 2.5". USA. 1960s. Screw tops. © Walt Disney Productions. $40-50.

Tinker Bell. 2.5". Japan. 1960s. © Walt Disney Productions. Screw tops. $25-30.

Tinker Bell. 2.5". Manufactured by Eleanore Welborn Art Productions Inc., Monterey, CA, COPR 1955, Walt Disney Productions. Screw tops. $90-100.

Pinocchio

Pinocchios. 5". Japan. 1960s. $125-150.

Pinocchios. 5". Japan. 1940s. $125-150.

Pinocchio and the Dutch girl from the movie "Pinocchio." 4.75". Japan. 1940s. $125-150.

Pinocchios. 4.5". USA. 1960s. Chalkware. $40-50.

Pinocchios. 2.75"-3". Japan. 1950s. $65-75.

Pinocchio and Geppetto. 3.25". Taiwan. 1990s. Danbury Mint. $45-50.

Pinocchio and the Dutch girl. 3". Country unknown. 1990s. New England Collectors Society. $50-55.

Pinocchio and Jiminy Cricket condiment. 4.25".
Japan. 1940s. Bought in Japan in 1946 by an
American soldier in the occupation Army. Ex-
tremely rare, $500+.

Pinocchio and Jiminy Cricket. 5". Japan. 1950s. $200+.

Pinocchio and Jiminy Cricket. 3.25". Japan. 1950s. Note don-
key ears on Pinocchio. $175+.

Jiminy Cricket. 3". USA. 1950s. Chalkware. $75-85.

Figaros. 3.5". Japan. 1950s. $65-75.

Figaros kissing and apart, 3.5". Japan. 1960s. $65-75.

Figaro condiment. 4.5". Japan. 1950s. Red and gold label Fairyland China. Note: small head in mustard is spoon end. $250+.

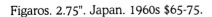

Figaros. 2.75". Japan. 1960s $65-75.

Figaros. 4.25". American Bisque Co., U.S.A. 1960s. $225-250.

Figaro on basket. 4". Goebel, Germany. 1950s. Licensed by Walt Disney Productions. Mold numbers DIS 138A&B. Rare. 400+.

Figaros. 4". No mark, flat unglazed bottom, probably U.S.A. 1940s. $100-125.

"Figaro and Cleo." Licensed U.S.A. 1960s. $65-75.

Schiffer Publishing Ltd.

☐ hardcover
☐ paperback

TITLE OF BOOK: _____

   ☐ Bought at: _____
   ☐ Received as gift

COMMENTS: _____
_____
_____
_____

Name *(please print clearly)* _____

Address _____

City _____ State _____ Zip _____

☐ *Please send me a free Schiffer Arts, Antiques & Collectibles catalog.*

☐ *Please send me a free Schiffer Woodcarving, Woodworking & Crafts catalog*

☐ *Please send me a free Schiffer Military/Aviation History catalog*

☐ *Please send me a free Whitford Press Mind, Body & Spirit and Donning Pictorials &*
   Cookbooks catalog.

SCHIFFER BOOKS ARE CURRENTLY AVAILABLE FROM YOUR BOOKSELLER

Figaros. 3". USA. 1941-42. National Porcelain Co., © WDP. $75-85.

Figaros. 3". National Porcelain Co., Trenton, NJ. 1941-42. © WDP faintly incised on back. Produced in the four colors shown. $75-85.

Figaros. 3" Probably USA. 1940s. $55-65.

Cleos. 2.75"-3.25". Japan. 1950s. $50-60.

Cleos. 2.75". USA. 1950s. Private ceramicist. $30-40.

101 Dalmatians. 4". Taiwan. 1990s. © Disney. $30-35.

101 Dalmatians. 4.25". USA. 1990s. © Disney. Treasure Craft. $25-30.

Pocahontas and Meeko. 4". Mexico. 1995. © Disney. Treasure Craft. $25-30.

Pocahontas. 3.75". USA 1990s. T.C. © Disney. Sold at Disneyland. $15-20.

Pocahontas and John Smith. 3". USA. 1995. © Disney. Treasure Craft. $18-20.

Seabees and Phoebee. 3". USA. 1940s. Mascot for US Navy Seabees (Navy Construction Battalions). WWII Disney art. $40-50.

Snow White and the Seven Dwarfs. She is 4.5". Dwarfs are 3.25".
USA. 1950s. Chalkware. Complete set. $375+.

Snow White napkin holder with Doc and Dopey shakers. 5.75".
Gift Gallery. Japan. © Walt Disney Productions MCMLXIV.
$225+.

Snow White. 3.5". Japan. 1950s. $65-75.

Snow White kissing Dopey. 4". China. 1990s. © Disney. $25-30.

Snow White and the Wicked Queen. 3.25". Taiwan. 1990s. Danbury Mint. $45-50.

Snow White and Witch. 4.5". USA. 1990s. Rick Wisecarver, Ohio. $60-70.

Snow White. 4.25". 1970s. T.C. USA © Walt Disney Productions. $100+.

Dopey and Grumpy. 4.5". Concessione S.A. Creazioni Walt Disney. Made in Italy. 1970s. Artist signed. Rare, $400+.

Grumpy and Happy. 5.25". Japan. 1960s. $125-150.

The Seven Dwarfs. 2.75". Foreign (Japan). 1940s. $100-125 pair.

Dwarf heads. 3". Japan. 1950s. $100-125, pair.

Sneezy

Dopey

Bashful

Happy

Doc

Grumpy

The Seven Dwarfs (five shown). 3.5-3.75". Incised Mexico. Early 1940s. $150+ pair.

Dopeys. 2.75". Japan. 1950s. $65-75.

Sneezy and Grumpy. 3.75". Japan. 1990s. © Walt Disney Company. Available only at Tokyo Disneyland. $135-150.

Happy and Dopey. 4". Japan. 1950s. $65-75.

Happy and Sleepy condiment. 2.5". Wadeheath by permission Walt Disney, England. 1930s. Rare, $500+.

Sneezy and Bashful. 5". USA. 1990s. © Disney. Treasure Craft. $35-40.

Dopey and Grumpy. 2.5". Japan. 1960s. $125.

The Three Little Pigs

Fifer & Fiddler pigs. 3.5". Japan. 1960s. $65-75.

·Fifer, Fiddler, and Practical Pig. 2.75". Germany. 1930s. $400+.

Fifer type pigs. 3.5". Japan. 1950s. $65-75.

The Three Little Pigs. 3". Country unknown. 1990s. New England Collectors Society. $50-55.

The Three Little Pigs. 3.5". Japan. 1940s. Borgfeldt, licensed Disney. $200+.

Fifer and Fiddler pigs. 2.75". Japan. 1930s. $65-75.

Pigs from Silly Symphony. 3". Japan. $40-45.

The Big Bad Wolf with one pig hiding in a hut. 4". Probably USA. Gold label Meridam. 1960s. $75-85.

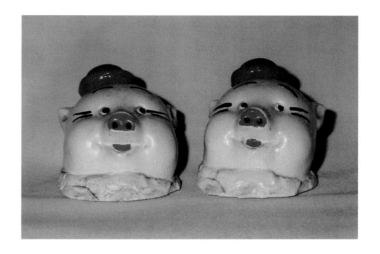

Practical Pig. 2". USA. 1940s. Chalkware. $65-75.

The Big Bad Wolf and The Three Little Pigs from the movies of the same name. 3.75". China. 1992. Issued by Albert E. Price, Inc. $10-12.

Three Little Pigs and the Wolf. 4.5". China. 1990s. Issued by Enesco with matching cookie jar. $15-18.

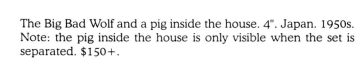

The Big Bad Wolf and a pig inside the house. 4". Japan. 1950s. Note: the pig inside the house is only visible when the set is separated. $150+.

Fifer and Fiddler pig condiment. 4". Japan. 1930s. Marutomo Ware. $175-200.

Three Little Pigs condiment. 3.5". Japan. 1950s. $175-200.

Three Little Pigs condiment. 4.75". Japan. 1950s. Blue and silver Royal Sealy label. Note: small head in mustard is spoon end. $250+.

Fifer and Fiddler pig condiments. 3.5". Japan. 1930s. Second set, Marutomo Ware. $175-200.

Winnie the Pooh and Friends

Winnie the Pooh and the hunny pot. 2.75". Country unknown. 1990s. New England Collectors Society. $50-55.

Winnie and the hunny pot. 3". Malaysia. 1990s. © Disney. $25-30.

Winnie on balloon. 3". Japan. 1990s. © Disney. $35-40.

Pooh Chefs. 3". Japan. 1990s. © Walt Disney Company, K. Onishi M.D.Co.Ltd. Sold at Tokyo Disneyland. White glass. $30-35.

Winnie the Pooh holiday. 4.5". China. © Disney. Issued by the Disney store. $35-40.

Winnie and the hunny pot. 4". Mexico. 1990s. Treasure Craft. © Disney. $20-25.

Winnie and Tigger. 4.25". China. 1990s. © Disney. $35-40.

Kanga and Roo from "Winnie the Pooh and the Honey Tree." 5". Japan. © MCMLXIV Walt Disney Prod. Enesco $150-175.

Piglet and Eeyore. 4.5". Mexico. 1990s. Treasure Craft © Disney. $20-25.

Winnie on Eeyore. 4". Japan. 1990s. © Disney. $35-40.

Owl from "Winnie the Pooh." 3.25". Japan. 1960s. $65-75.

Winnie and Piglet. 4". Mexico. 1990s. © Disney. Treasure Craft. $25-30.

Famous Walt Disney Character salt and pepper
sets on tray. © Walt Disney Productions. Enesco. Japan. 4". 1960s. $250+ each set.

Dopey and Snow White.　　　Donald Duck and a nephew.

Pluto and Mickey Mouse.　　　　　　　　Winnie the Pooh and Rabbit.

Pinocchio and Jiminy Cricket.　　Thumper and Bambi.

HANNA-BARBERA

Tom and Jerry from "Puss Gets the Boot," the first cartoon created by William Hanna and Joseph Barbera while at MGM.

Tom and Jerry. 3". Marked Foreign (probably Japan). 1960s. 200+.

Tom and Jerry condiment from the comic strip of the same name. 3.5". Japan. 1960s. $300+.

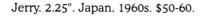

Jerry. 2.25". Japan. 1960s. $50-60.

Tom

Characters from MGM Studios. 1.5-2.25". Japan. 1950s. $90-100, pair.

Droopy Dog

Screwey Squirrel

Pepe

Barney Bear from "The Bear that Couldn't Sleep."

Spike

The Jetsons, George and Jane, premiered in 1962. 4.5". Probably Japan. 1991, one of 12 prototypes produced by Vandor. The design was not approved for production. Extremely rare. Unpriced.

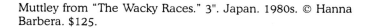

Muttley from "The Wacky Races." 3". Japan. 1980s. © Hanna Barbera. $125.

Pixie and Dixie from "Huckleberry Hound." (Or perhaps this is Jerry? Some people think so.) 3". Japan. 1960s. $50-60.

The Flintstones

The first episode of "The Flintstones" premiered on ABC in September, 1960, featuring Fred and Wilma Flintstone and their neighbors Barney and Betty Rubble. They lived in the town of Bedrock, Cobblestone County, located 250 miles below sea level. Pebbles was born in early 1963 and Bamm-Bamm was found on the Rubbles doorstep later that year. Dino was the pet dinosaur.

Fred Flintstone and Barney Rubble. 4.5". Probably USA. 1960s. Incised © HBP. $175+.

Bamm-Bamm Rubble and Pebbles Flintstone. 4". Probably USA. 1960s. Incised © HBP. $175+.

The Flintstones. 3.5"-5.5". China. 1990s. © Hanna Barbera Productions Inc. Issued by Certified International Corp. (CIC), New York. $20-25.

Fred and Barney in lodge hats.

Fred and Barney.

Fred cookout.

Pebbles and Bamm Bamm.

Fred pushing Pebbles.

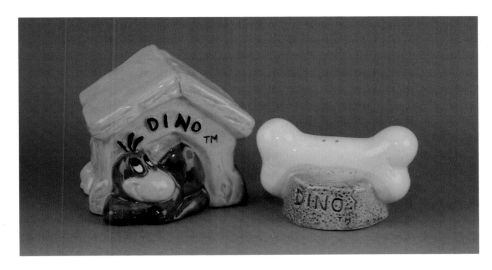

Dino and his bone.

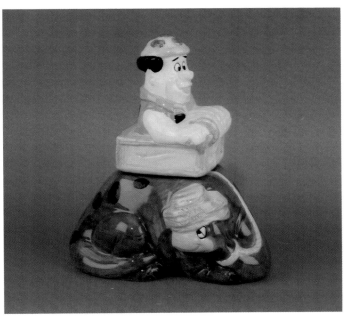

Fred riding Dino.

Fred and Wilma Flintstone. 4.25". Japan. 1989. Issued by Vandor. Licensed Hanna Barbera. After set was issued, the licensor ordered the remaining stock destroyed. $75-85.

Pebbles and Bamm-Bamm. 4.25". Korea. 1990s. Issued by Harry James Ltd, England. $75-85.

Pebbles, Bamm-Bamm and Dino. 4.5". Japan. 1970s. Composition material. Licensed. Sold at Bedrock City, Custer, South Dakota. $50-60.

Pebbles and Bamm Bamm. 4". Korea. 1990. © Hanna Barbera Productions Inc. Vandor. $35-40.

Pebbles and Bamm-Bamm. 4.25". Japan. © 1985, issued by Vandor in 1989. $75-85.

Flintstones, Bedrock City, Kelowma B.C., Canada. 2.75". Japan. © Hanna Barbera Productions Inc. 74. Shown are Fred with Pebbles and Wilma. $50-60.

Flintstones, Bedrock City, Custer So.Dak. 5.25". Probably USA. 1960s. Shown are Bamm-Bamm, Pebbles, and Dino. $75.

Fred and Barney, Bedrock City, Grand Canyon, Arizona. 2.75". Japan. 1980s. © 1977 HBP, front and back views. $75.

WARNER BROTHERS

The founders of the Warner Brothers Studio started at the same time and place as Walt Disney—Kansas City, in the early 1920s. To promote their cartoons, they needed a tie-in to the music from WB feature length films, so "Looney Tunes" began in 1930 with "Sinking in the Bathtub." "Gold Diggers of 49," released in 1936, was the first appearance for Porky Pig. Daffy Duck followed the next year in "Porky's Duck Hunt" as did Elmer Fudd. It was 1940 in "Wild Hare" when Bugs Bunny debuted with his famous "Eh, What's up Doc?" He was followed by Tweety Bird in "Tale of Two Kitties," 1942; Yosemite Sam in "Hare Trigger," 1944; Foghorn Leghorn in "Walky Talky Hawky," 1946; Sylvester the Cat, with Tweety, in "Tweety Pie," 1947; Pepe LePew in "The Odorable Kitty," 1947; and the Roadrunner and Wile E. Coyote in the 1948 "Fast and Furry-ous." Mel Blanc created and portrayed the voices of many Warner Brothers characters.

Porky Pig as a cobbler with a boot. 4". Japan. 1950s. $75-85.

Porky in a wheelbarrow. 4". Japan. 1950s. $100-125.

Porky & Petunia. 5". USA. 1950s. American Pottery Co. $100-125.

Porky Pigs. 5". USA. 1950s. American Pottery Co. $75-85 pair.
Gold trim. $100-125.

Porky and Petunia. 5". China. © 94 WB. $45-50.

Porky and Petunia hugging letters. 2.5".
USA. 1950s. $35-40.

Petunia on a scale. 4.25". Japan. 1950s. $100-125.

Petunia on a scale. 4.5". Philippines. 1989. Vandor. $15-20.

First issue of Looney Tunes characters. 4". Japan. 1970s. © Warner Bros. Distributed by both Lego Imports, USA and Enterprise Sales and Distributors Ltd., Toronto, Canada. Of this series, Tweety is the hardest set to find, $225-250. Other sets, $150-175.

Tweety Bird

Bugs Bunny

Sylvester the Cat

Yosemite Sam

Sylvester. 4.5". China. 1993. Prototype, not issued by (CIC). $75-100.

Sylvester and Tweety. 4.5". China. © 93 Warner Bros. Issued by CIC. Different from prototype in eyes, whiskers, and bottom. $20-25.

Sylvester and Tweety on Christmas ornaments. 2.5". China. 1990s. © Warner Bros. Inc. $25-30.

Sylvester and Tweety. 4.5". Taiwan. 1990s. Licensed WB. Issued by Applause Inc. $30-35.

Sylvester and Tweety dinner. 3". Taiwan. 1990s. © Warner Bros. Inc. $25-30.

Sylvester and Tweety. 5.5". China. © 94 WB. $45-50.

Granny, Sylvester, and Tweety. 6.5". China. 1990s. © Warner Brothers. $35-40.

Left: Sylvester and Tweety Tourist. 5". Thailand. © 94 WB. $35-40.

Sylvester and Tweety. 5". China. © 93 Warner Bros. Issued by CIC. $20-25.

Left: Spike and Sylvester. 5". China. 1990s. © Warner Bros. Inc. $35-40.

Tweety on cage. 3.75". Taiwan. © 1994 Warner Bros. Inc. Issued by Six Flags Theme Parks. $30-35.

Sylvester and Tweety in birdcages. 3". China. 1990s. $25-30.

Tweety. 3.75". China. 1993. Prototype, not produced by CIC. $125-150.

Tweety. 3.25". Japan. 1960s. © Kreiss. $35-40.

Tweety. 2.75". Probably Japan. 1980. © Warner Bros., Inc. $50-60.

Two Bugs sharing a carrot. 4". USA. 1960s. Treasure Craft. $40-50.

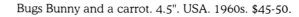

Bugs and engine in "The Flaming Carrot" car. 6". China. © 94 WB. $45-50.

Bugs Bunny and a carrot. 4.5". USA. 1960s. $45-50.

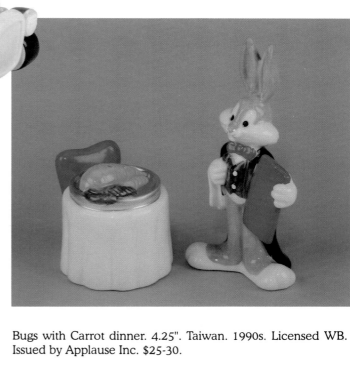

Bugs with Carrot dinner. 4.25". Taiwan. 1990s. Licensed WB. Issued by Applause Inc. $25-30.

Carmen Miranda Bugs. 6.5". China. © 95 WB. $35-40.

Left: Bugs and Honey Bunny. 6.75". China. © 94 WB. $35-40.

Above: Bugs and Yosemite Sam. 5.75". China. © 93 Warner Bros. Issued by CIC. $20-25.

Left: Bugs Bunny and Elmer Fudd. 6.5". China. © 94 WB. $45-50.

Above: Bugs and Gossamer. 6.75". China. 1990s. © Warner Brothers. $35-40.

Left: Bugs and Elmer Fudd. 5.25". China. © 93 Warner Bros. Issued by CIC. $20-25.

Right: Bugs and Tasmanian Devil Football. 5.5". China. © 93 Warner Bros. Issued by CIC. $20-25.

Above: Bugs and Daffy Duck. 5". China. © 93 Warner Bros. Issued by CIC. $20-25.

Right: Tas and Bugs. 4.5". China. 1993. Prototype, not produced by CIC. $125-150.

Above: Bugs and Daffy Duck. 5.5". China. © 93 Warner Bros. Issued by CIC. $20-25.

Right: Bugs and Tas Baseball. 5.5". China. © 93 Warner Bros. Issued by CIC. $20-25.

Bugs and Tas prototype. 4". China. 1990s. Not produced by CIC. $150+.

Left: Bugs and Tas Christmas. 5.25". China. © 93 Warner Bros. Issued by CIC. $20-25.

Bugs holding carrot. 5". China. 1990s. © Warner Bros. Inc. $35-40.

Left: Tas couch potato and Bugs in TV. 4". China. © 95 WB. $35-40.

Tas. 4". Taiwan. 1990s. © Warner Bros. Issued by Applause Inc. $30-35.

Left: Tas and refrigerator. 3". Taiwan. 1990s. © Warner Bros. $25-30.

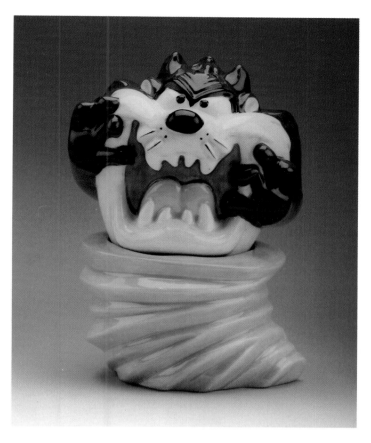

Tas with motorcycle. 5". China. © 94 WB. $45-50.

Tas in a tornado. 5.25". China. 1990s. $35-40.

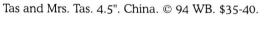

Tas and Mrs. Tas. 4.5". China. © 94 WB. $35-40.

"Wedding Bliss," Tas and Mrs. Tas. 5.5". China. © 95 WB. $35-40.

Tasmanian Devil/National Football League. 3.5". China. © 1994 National Football League Properties (NFLP) and © 94 WB. Issued by CIC. $18-20.

Arizona Cardinals and San Francisco 49ers.

Dallas Cowboys and New York Giants.

Miami Dolphins and Buffalo Bills.

Green Bay Packers and Chicago Bears.

Pittsburgh Steelers and New York Jets.

Oakland Raiders and Kansas City Chiefs.

Pepe LePew and Penelope. 5'. China. © 94 WB. $35-40.

Pepe. 3". Taiwan. 1990s. Issued by Applause Inc. Licensed WB. $25-30.

Foghorn Leghorn, Henry Hawk, and Barney. 6". China. 1990s. © Warner Brothers. $35-40.

Foghorn Leghorn and Henry Hawk. 5". China. © 93 Warner Bros. Issued by CIC. $20-25.

Foghorn and Barney. 5". China. 1990s. © Warner Bros. Inc. $35-40.

Foghorn with egg. 4.5". Taiwan. 1990s. Licensed WB. Issued by Applause Inc. $30-35.

Marvin the Martian. 3.75". Sri Lanka. © 94 Warner Bros. Issued by Applause Inc. $25-30.

Marvin the Martian. 4". China. © 93 Warner Bros. Issued by CIC. $20-25.

Marvin and K-9. 4.5". China. © 95 WB. $35-40.

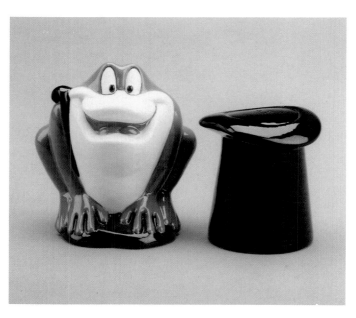

Michigan J. Frog. 4.5". China. 1990s. © Warner Brothers. $35-40.

Marc Antony and Pussyfoot. 4". China 1990s. © Warner Bros. Inc. $35-40.

Wile E. Coyote and Road Runner. 5.5". China. © 93 Warner Bros. Issued by CIC. $20-25.

Wile E. and Road Runner TNT. 5.25". China. © 93 Warner Bros. Issued by CIC. $20-25.

Wile E. and Road Runner. 3". China. 1990s. © WB. $35-40.

Pinky and the Brain from Animaniacs. 5.75". Thailand. © WB 94. $35-40.

Looney Tunes characters. 3.75". Taiwan. 1993. Issued by CIC, © Warner Bros. $18-20.

Sylvester and Tweety, Sylvester and Pepe. 3". Canada. 1990s. Licensed WB. $12-15.

Bugs and Tas, Wile E. and Road Runner. 3". Canada. 1990s. Licensed WB. $12-15.

Sylvester and Tweety diner. 3". Canada. 1990s. Licensed WB. $12-15.

WALTER LANTZ

The Walter Lantz Studio started in 1928 with a redesigned Oswald the Rabbit, a character originated by Disney. Andy Panda was created in 1938. Woody Woodpecker joined Andy in "Knock" in 1940. Chilly Willy was designed in 1953.

Woody Woodpecker

Woody Woodpecker and His Friends Salt and Peppers. A series, © 1958, Walter Lantz Productions Inc., Licensed Exclusively to National Potteries, Cleveland, Ohio. 4". Japan. $200+, pair.

Wally Walrus & Windy Bear

Original package

Andy & Miranda Panda

Homer Pigeon & Charlie Chicken

Chilly Willy & Oswald Rabbit

Splinter & Knothead, Woody's nephews

Woody & Winnie Woodpecker

Woody & Winnie. 5.75". Probably Korea. W. Lantz © 1990. Issued by Sarsaparilla Deco Designs Ltd, NJ. Sold primarily at Universal Studio. $75-85.

Woody Woodpecker. 3.75". USA. 1960s. © WLC. $125+.

Woody Woodpecker. 3". Probably USA. 1960s. $75-85.

Li'l Eight Ball. 3.5". USA. 1950s. A label we saw on a figurine says © Lantz Productions, Eight Ball, Made by Don Roberto, Los Angeles. $200+.

Sniffles. 3.25". USA. 1950s. $200+.

FOREIGN CHARACTERS

Adamson. 3.5". Germany. 1930s. Goebel. European cartoon character. Shown with and without hat and jacket. $90-100.

Adamson. 3.25-3.75". Japan. 1950s. Left set, $65-75. Right set, $40-50.

Big Ears and Noddy from the English comic strip "Noddy" by Enid Blyton. 3.5". England. 1950s. $250+.

Astro Boy and Girl. 3". Japan. 1980s. Japanese comic characters. © Tezuka Production. Issued by Shin & Company. $150-175.

Dismal Desmond condiment. 3". Germany. 1930s. Dismal
Desmond was a British comic strip character in the 1920s-1930s.
$175-200.

Dismal Desmond. 3". Japan. 1950s. $75-85.

Kewpies were created by author and artist Rose O'Neill. Kewpie illustrations first appeared in the *Ladies Home Journal* in 1909. They also were in a Sunday comic strip in the mid-1930s. The original Kewpies were bisque, primarily nude, unisex, had molded hair in a "topknot" and were made in Germany.

Kewpies

Kewpies with rabbits, pumpkin, chicks, turkey and clover. Each shaker represents a month of the year. Reg U.S. Patent Office. Top two sets, 1.75"; other sets, 2.5". Germany. 1930s. Probably sold mix and match. $500+ pair.

Kewpies. First set, 1.75". Japan. 1940s. Porcelain. $75-100. Second set, 1.5". Japan. 1940s. Ceramic. $50-60.

Kewpie condiment. 4". Germany. 1930s. $250+.

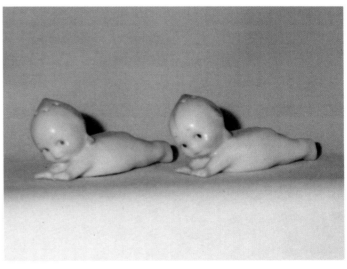

Kewpies, set on box 1.75". Occupied Japan (only box marked). 1940s. Porcelain. $75-100. Other set 2". Japan. 1950s. Ceramic. $50-60.

Kewpies reclining. 1". Germany. 1930s. $350+.

Kewpies. 2.5". Probably USA. 1940s. Silver plate with a large cork. $150+.

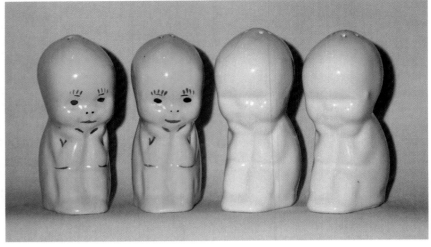

Kewpies. Left set 3.25". $85-100. Other sets 3.5". $50-60. All USA.
1950s.

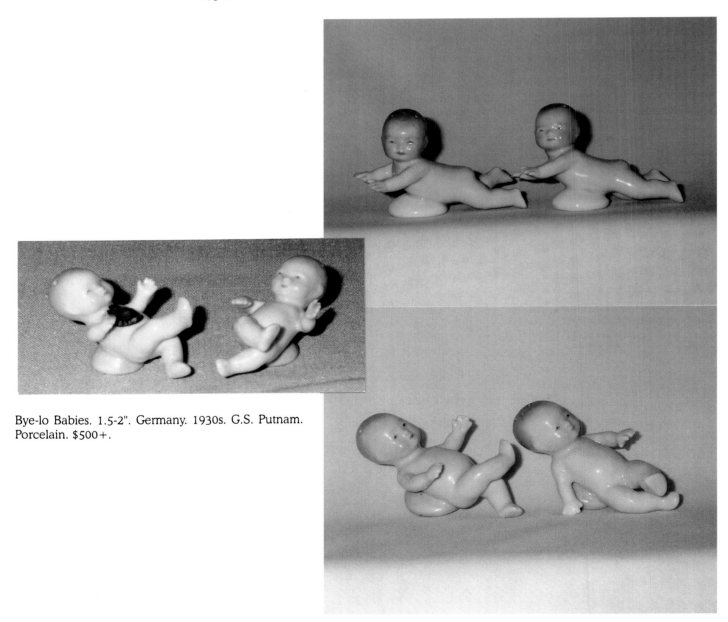

Bye-lo Babies. 1.5-2". Germany. 1930s. G.S. Putnam.
Porcelain. $500+.

Bonzo

Created by George Studdy, Bonzo was introduced about 1912 in the British paper *The Sketch*, in a supporting role. Over the next ten years, his appearance changed from a realistic white bull terrier into the button-nosed, fat-footed, floppy-eared creature that became a national mascot. Officially named Bonzo in 1922, he starred in 25 animated cartoons during 1924-25. He also appeared as a weekly comic strip in America.

Bonzos. 3.25". Probably USA. 1950s. Pink pair and blue single. $30-40 pair.

Bonzos. 2.75". USA. 1950s. $35-40.

Bonzos. 2.75". Japan. 1950s. $25-30.

Bonzos. Left set 2.75". USA. 1950s. $40-50. Right set 2". Japan. 1960s. $20-25.

Bonzos. 3". Occupied Japan. 1940s. $35-40.

Bonzos. 2.5"-2.75". Left set Japan. Right
set USA. 1950s. $25-30.

Bonzos. 3". Japan. 1950s. $30-35.

Bonzos. 3". Japan. 1950s. $35-40.

Bonzos. 3". Japan. 1950s. $30-35.

Bonzos. 2.75". Japan. 1950s. Left set, $30-35. Right set, $25-30.

Bonzos. 3". Probably USA. 1950s. Left set, $35-40. Right set, $55-60.

Bonzos. 3". Japan. 1950s. $40-45.

Bonzos. 2.25"-2.75". USA. 1940s. National Porcelain Co. $50-55.

Bonzos. 3" & 2.5". Japan. 1950s. Lustreware. $55-60.

Bonzos. 3.25". Japan. 1950s. $45-50.

Bonzos. 2.75". Germany. 1930s. $90-100.

Bonzos. 2.25". Japan. 1950s. $35-40.

Bonzos. 2.75". Japan. 1950s. $45-50.

Bonzo. 2.75". Germany. 1930s. $45-50/single.

Bonzos. 2.75". Japan. 1950s. $55-60.

Bonzos. 2.75". Stamped USA. 1950s. Chalkware. $40-45.

Bonzo condiment. 3.5". Japan. 1950s. $60-70.

Bonzo condiments. 3.25". Japan. 1950s. Lustreware. $90-100.

Bonzo condiment. 3". Germany. 1930s. "Foreign" incised on the back of base. $175+.

Bonzo condiment. 4". Japan. 1960s. $125+.

Bonzo mustard with S&P cats condiment. 3.25". Germany. 1930s. Transfer (scene painted on china) of "A present from Forth Bridge" (Scotland). $175+.

Bonzo condiment. 3.5". Germany. 1930s. $200+.

Bonzo with cats condiment. 3.5". Germany. 1930s. $200+.

Bonzo condiments. Tongue is the mustard spoon.

4". Japan. 1950s. Trico Nagoya. $90-100.

3.25". Japan. 1960s. $75-85.

4". Japan. 1950s. Lustreware. $75-85.

3". Japan. 1960s. Lustreware. $75-85.

3.75". Japan. 1950s. Lustreware. $90-100.

2.75". Japan. 1960s. Lustreware. $90-100.

David the Gnome from the cartoon of the same name. Shown with his granddaughter, a rabbit, and a chipmunk. 4". Japan. © 1979 Unieboek B.V. (Netherlands). Imported by Quon-Quon. $65-75

Paddington Bear. 4". Japan. 1980s. © Eden Toys Inc. 1978. Tag says "Darkest Peru to London England, via Paddington Station," "Please look after this bear." $200+.

PiYo PiYo, Japanese comic character. Salt, mustard, and toothpick condiment. 3". Japan. © 1991. Tung Ling Company design. $50-60.

PiYo PiYo. 3.5". Japan. 1980s. Incised Tokai. Duck has squealer in base. $50-60.

Pip, Squeak & Wilfred

Pip, Squeak & Wilfred. First issued in 1919 in the Great Britain *Daily Mirror*, this comic about Pip (a mongrel dog), Squeak (a grown penguin) and Wilfred (a baby rabbit) was so popular it lasted until the mid-1950s. Anthropomorphic and domesticated, they lived with their folks on the edge of London near the country. Their appeal was so great that the Wilfredian League of Gugnuncs was founded in 1927, soon numbering 100,000 members, raising money for children's hospitals and charities. The name came from Wilfred who said only "Gug" (baby-talk) and "Nunc" for Uncle. This collectors' group is still in existence.

Pip, Squeak, and Wilfred condiment. 2.75". Germany. 1930s. $250+.

Squeak. 3.25". Germany. 1930s. $90-100.

Pip, Squeak and Wilfred condiment. 3.5". England. 1940s. $250+.

Pip, Squeak, and Wilfred condiment. 4.5". Germany. 1930s. Transfer of Danzig Artushof (Poland). $250+.

Pip, Squeak, and Wilfred condiment. 4.5". Germany. 1930s. $200+.

Squeak condiments. 3-3.75". Germany. 1930s. $200+.

Wilfred condiments. 3.5". Germany. 1930s. $150+.

VARIOUS U.S. CHARACTERS

Betty Boop, created by Grim Natwick for Fleischer Studio in 1930, made her debut in Dizzy Dishes. Bimbo, later featured as her dog, appeared first. Betty looked more like a dog than a person in her early cartoons, but her dog ears became earrings as she was changed into a flirtatious vamp.

Betty Boop

Betty Boop poolside. 4.5". Taiwan. 1994. © King Features. Vandor. $45-50.

Betty Boop Oscar. 5.75". Indonesia. 1994. Licensed, Vandor. $18-20.

Betty and car. 3.75". Indonesia. 1994. Licensed, Vandor. $18-20.

Betty Boop chef. 5". Taiwan. 1995. © King Features. Vandor. $20-25.

Betty Boop holiday. 4". Indonesia. 1994. Licensed, Vandor. $18-20.

Betty Boop with camera. 3". Taiwan. 1995. © King Features. Vandor. $25-30.

Betty Boop. 4.75". Taiwan. © 1995. KFS Inc/FS Inc. Benjamin and Medwin Inc. $15-18.

Betty Boop and Bimbo on napkin holder. 5". Japan. 1990. Issued by Vandor. © KFS. $100-125.

Betty Boop Tropico. 3". Taiwan. © 1992 KFS/FS. Vandor. $18 - 20.

Betty and Bimbo. 3.5". Philippines. 1980s. Licensed, Vandor. $30-35.

Skater Boop and Bimbo. 4.5". Philippines. 1992. Licensed, Vandor. $30-35.

Bimbo holding a stack of books. 2.5". USA. 1930s. $150+.

Ken and Barbie. 4". China. 1990s. © Mattel Inc. Enesco. $20-25.

Barbies. 5". Japan. 1960s. $65-75.

Casper. 6". USA. 1990s. Incised on back Harvey Comics, private ceramicist. $125-150.

Casper. 4". Mexico. 1996. Produced by Treasure Craft for Star Jars. Unpainted clay model. $35-40.

Maggie & Jiggs

Maggie & Jiggs. 2.25". Japan. 1940s.
$125-150.

Maggie & Jiggs from "Bringing Up Father". 3.25". Germany.
1930s. Stamped Cop.P.S. $200+.

Maggie & Jiggs. 2.25". Left set Japan.
1950s. $125-150. Right set Germany.
1930s. $150-175.

Maggie & Jiggs. 2.5". Japan. 1950s.
Lustreware. $200+.

Maggie & Jiggs. 3.25". Germany. 1930s. Rare. $300+.

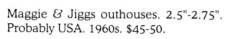

Maggie & Jiggs outhouses. 2.5"-2.75".
Probably USA. 1960s. $45-50.

Maggie & Jiggs on one shaker; Barney Google & Spark Plug
from "Barney Google" on the other. 2". Japan. 1940s. $100+.

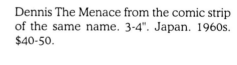

Dennis The Menace from the comic strip
of the same name. 3-4". Japan. 1960s.
$40-50.

Brother Juniper from the comic strip of the same name. Left set, 3.75". Right set, 3". Japan. 1970s. Brother Juniper was the first comic strip about a clergyman written by a clergyman, Father Justin McCarthy. Left set $65-75. Right set $40-50.

Brother Juniper. 3.5". Japan. 1960s. $12-15.

Brother Juniper. 3". Japan. 1960s. $12-15.

Cathy from comic strip of same name. Sets of Cathy with blonde hair are prototypes from CIC, never produced. Sets of Cathy with brown hair are slightly smaller and were produced in Sri Lanka for Papel Freelance in 1995, licensed by Guisewite Studio. Prototypes $125+. Other sets, $15-20.

Felix the Cat

Felix the Cat, star of the 1920 films *Feline Follies* and *Musical Mews*, also appeared in comic strips. Famous for his "walking" pose.

Felix. 2.5". Germany. 1920s. $350+.

Felix. 2.5". Germany. 1920s. $200+.

Felix. 2.25". Germany. 1930s. Glass eyes. $400+ pair.

Felix single. 2". Germany. 1930s. If a pair, $250+.

Felix. 3". Germany. 1940s. Movable eyes. Sold at Tiques Auction, 1994. $400+.

Felix type. 3.5". Japan. 1940s. $65-75.

Felix, 3". Japan. 1950s. $400+.

Gold Felix. 3". Japan. Rare. $400+.

Felix. 3". Japan. 1950s. Side and back views. $400+.

"Felix Keeps on Walking." 2.5". Germany. 1920s. Four digit number on bottom. Extremely rare. Sold at 'Tiques Auction in 1992 for $1,100.

Felix. 2.25". Japan. 1950s. $400+.

Felix condiment. 3.25". Germany. 1920s. Extremely rare. $800+.

Felix condiment. 3.75". Japan. 1940s. The spoon forms the tail of the mustard. $500+.

Felix. 3.5". Taiwan. 1990s. Initial prototype by Benjamin and Medwin Inc., NY. $150+.

Felix. 3.5". Probably Taiwan. 1994. Second prototype. $75-85.

Felix. 3.75". Taiwan. 1994. © Felix the Cat Productions Inc. Final production set. $15-18.

Hello Kitty. 2.75". Paper label, Japan. 1980. Gold label on back with name. © 1976 by Sanrio Surprises, distributed by Sanrio Co. Ltd. $85-100.

Garfield

All Garfield S&Ps were licensed by United Features Syndicate, Inc © 1978 and 1981. All but one set were issued by the Enesco Corp. of Illinois.

Chef Garfield and Garfield emerging from egg. Left set, 4". Japan. Right set, 3.25". Taiwan. 1980s. $90-100.

Garfield "Loose in the Kitchen." 3.5". Taiwan. 1990. Issued by Molly Houseware Ltd., England. $50-60.

Garfield's Cafe. 4". Taiwan. 1980s. $30-40.

Garfield chefs. 3". Taiwan. 1980s. Issued by Enesco. © 1978 UFS Inc. $65-75.

Garfield and Odie. 4". Taiwan. 1980s. $65-75.

Garfield and Arlene. 3.25". Korea. $80-90.

Stacking Thanksgiving and Halloween Garfields. 3.5"-4". 1994. Prototype sets not produced by Enesco. $250+, per set.

Santa Garfields. 4". Probably Japan. 1980s. $100-125.

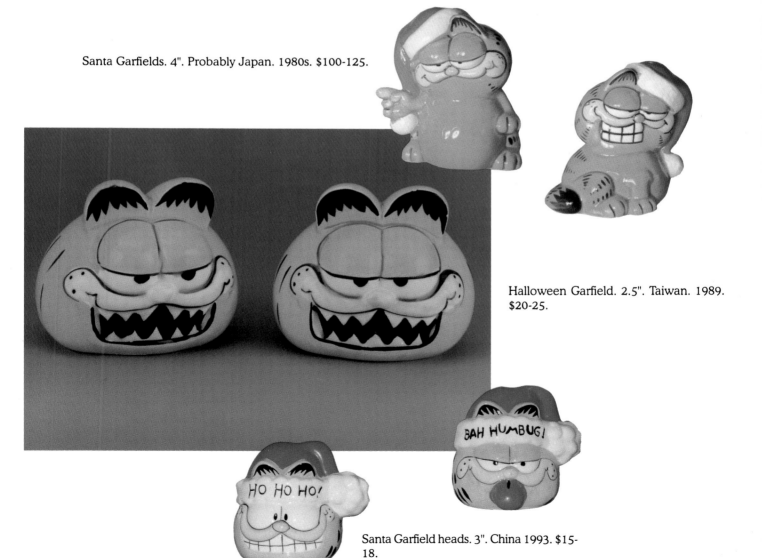

Halloween Garfield. 2.5". Taiwan. 1989. $20-25.

Santa Garfield heads. 3". China 1993. $15-18.

Andy and Min from "The Gumps." 4.25". Germany. 1930s. Shown out of and inside original box sewn in with thread. $250+.

Winnie Winkle and her brother Perry from the comic strip "Winnie Winkle the Breadwinner." 3.5". Germany. 1930s. $250+.

Chester & Andy Gump. 3.75". Germany. 1930s. $250+.

Uncle Walt (Walt Wallet) & Skeezix from "Gasoline Alley." 3.5". Germany. 1930s. $250+.

Happy Hooligan and Gloomy Gus condiment from "Happy Hooligan." 4.5". Germany. 1920s. Top is one piece S&P. $400+.

The Katzenjammer Kids/
The Captain and the Kids

The Katzenjammer Kids originated in the late 1800s with Rudolph Dirks of the *New York Journal.* The strip was based on the work of Wilhelm Busch, the German artist well known for his children's drawings. Named Hans & Fritz, they were called Katzenjammer, a German slang word for hangover. They were Mama's children; the Captain was an old sea dog who came to live with the family. Fifteen years later, Dirks went on a family vacation, precipitating problems with the Journal. He then went to

work for the *New York World,* but the strip title of K.K. remained with the *Journal,* as a result of a famous legal case. The new *World* comic was initially called Hans and Fritz; due to WWI, the title was changed to The Captain & the Kids. H.H. Knerr took over the K.K., licensed by King Features Syndicate (KFS), for the Journal. United Features Syndicate (UFS) licensed the World's Captain & the Kids. So two comic strips with two names by two artists in two papers, exactly the same characters!

The Captain and the Kids condiment. 3.5". Germany. 1930s. Porcelain. $600+.

Hans & Fritz. 2.5". Germany. 1930s. Porcelain. Although the same shakers as shown with the condiment, this set could have been sold separately. $250+.

Katzenjammer Kids. 3". Germany. 1959. Goebel, Liz Bulls. $500+.

Hans & Fritz. 3". Germany. 1930s. Goebel mold number DRGM 939536, incised crown, one-piece S&P. $500+.

Heckle and Jeckle from "The Talking Magpies," one of the Terrytoons. 3.25-3.5". Japan. 1970s. Set with feathers, Norcrest. Other sets Victoria Ceramics. $75-85.

Heckle and Jeckle-type. 4". Japan. 1970s. Artmark. $75-85.

Kliban. 2". Taiwan. 1970s. Shown with original box. $125-150.

Kliban emerging from egg. 3.75". Korea. 1970s. Designed by B.
Kliban and issued by Sigma the Taste Setter. $200+.

Kilban with victrola. 3.25". Japan. 1970s. Designed by B. Kilban
and issued by Sigma. $200+.

Kiko the Kangaroo (?) condiment from Terrytoons. 4.75". Japan. 1950s. As the other three condiments with red gloves known to date are character type sets, we believe this set also depicts a character. $150-175.

Pink Panther from the cartoon/movie of the same name. 3.5". Japan. © 1982 U.A. Tag says TM and © United Artists 1981 by Royal Orleans. Japan. $250+.

High Noon, from the cartoon "Cows of Moo Mesa." 3.75". Philippines. 1993. Clay Art. $20-25.

Li'l Abner

Mammy & Pappy Yokum. 4". Japan. 1950s. $200+.

Shmoos. 3.75". USA. 1950s. Imperial Porcelain. Also found with holes in back of the head. $200+.

Shmoos. 4". Japan. 1950s. $150+.

Shmoos. Left set 2". Blue Japan stamp with Japanese writing. 1940s. Porcelain. Right set 2.25". Japan. 1940s. $200+.

Shmoos. 3.5". USA. 1950s. Private ceramicist. $50-60.

Shmoos. Left set, 3.5". USA. 1940s. UFS, Inc. Al Capp, C. Pearce. $200+. Right set, 3". Probably USA. 1940s. $175.

Shmoos. USA. 1950s. Chalkware. Left set 3.5". $75-85. Right set 2.5". $50-60.

Shmoos. 3.5". Japan. 1950s. Incised Al Capp. $200+.

Dogpatch USA. The Shmoo. 2.75". Japan. 1970s. © Capp Enterprises Inc. $65-75.

Dogpatch USA. 2.75". Japan. Shown are Li'l Abner and Daisy Mae. © 1968 Capp Enterprises Inc. $65-75.

Dogpatch USA. Ceramic set on wooden tray. 2.75". Probably USA. 1970s. Shown are Li'l Abner, Daisy Mae, and Shmoo. $30-40. Plastic tea pot set. 2.5". Hong Kong. © 1975 Al Capp Enterprises. Label Dogpatch USA in the beautiful Ozarks. $25-30.

Dogpatch USA. 2". Hong Kong. Shown is Daisy Mae. Plastic. Capp Enterprises Inc. $25-30.

Max and Moritz. 3.5". Germany. 1930s. From the classic German picture-story of the same name by Wilhelm Busch in the late 1800s. $300+.

Max, Moritz, and their mother condiment. 3.25". Germany. 1930s. $500+.

Max and his mother. 1.75". Germany. 1930s. $125.

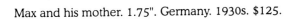

Mickey (Himself) McGuire from "Toonerville Folks." 3". Japan.
1940s. $40-50.

Nancy and Sluggo from "Nancy." 3.75".
Mexico. 1950s. Nancy joined the Fritzi Ritz
cartoon in 1933, Sluggo in 1938, then became a separate strip. Terrytoons also produced three cartoon shorts in the 1940s.
Each shaker has six holes in the back of
their shirts. $125-150.

Mutt & Jeff from the comic strip of the same name. 3.25". Germany. Incised © 1922 by Fisher & Fisher. $250+.

Moon Mullins, Kayo & Emmy Schmaltz (Lady Plushbottom) from
"Moon Mullins." 3.5". Germany. 1930s. $250+.

Peanuts

Charlie Brown and Lucy. 4". Taiwan. 1994. © 1950, 1966 United Feature Syndicate Inc. Benjamin and Medwin Inc. $15-18.

Charlie Brown and Lucy. 4.25". Korea. 1990. © 1950, 1966, United Features Syndicate Inc. $75-85.

Snoopy. 4.25". Japan. 1970s. Composition material. $20-25.

Snoopy hugging letters. 2.5". Japan. 1970s. $75-85.

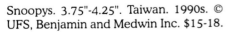

Snoopys. 3.75"-4.25". Taiwan. 1990s. © UFS, Benjamin and Medwin Inc. $15-18.

Snoopy and Woodstock. 4.5". Japan. 1960s. © 1958, 1966, United Features Syndicate Inc. $40-45.

Woodstock 3.75". Taiwan. 1994. 1950, 1966 United Feature Syndicate Inc. Benjamin and Medwin Inc. $15-18.

Popeye

Popeye was introduced in Thimble Theatre in 1929. This comic strip began in the early 1920s with Olive Oyl, her brother Castor, and her father Cole. The character Wimpy was based on a real life boxing referee whose frequent unpopular decisions were booed by the crowd. Popeye was also featured as the recruiting officer in special Navy comic strips during WWII.

Popeye and Sweet Pea. 3.5". Japan. 1980. © 1980 King Features Syndicate Inc. $150-175.

Popeye and Olive Oyl. 6.75"-7.25". Left set, Japan. 1980. Right set, Korea. 1990. Issued by Vandor. © 1980 KFS (King Features Syndicate). Most significant difference is in the size of Popeye's hat. Left set $125-150. Right set $90-100.

Popeyes. 2.75". Japan. 1950s. $100-125.

Popeye. 5". Taiwan. © 1995 KFS Inc/FS. Benjamin and Medwin Inc. $18-20.

Popeyes. 4". Japan. 1950s. $100-125.

Popeye condiment. 4.5". Japan. 1950s. $500+.

Popeye condiment. 4". Japan. 1950s. Only the boat is lustreware. $500+.

Popeye and Olive Oyl. 6.25". Japan. 1970s. Composition material. $65-75.

Popeye and Olive Oyl. 4.5". Taiwan. 1990s. $45-50.

Popeye and Olive Oyl. 2.5-3". Japan. Left set $200+. Right set $150+.

Wimpy and a hamburger. 2.5". Probably USA. 1960s. $75-85.

Wimpy. 2.75". Probably USA. 1960s. Glass with plastic hats. Originally sold filled with candy. $45-50.

Rudolph the Red Nosed Reindeer

Created in 1939 by Robert May, the original comic book was given as a premium by Montgomery Ward stores. The song was released in 1949 and the animated hour-long yuletide classic in 1964.

Rudolph the Red-Nosed Reindeer. 2.75". Japan. 1970s. Lefton. $30-35.

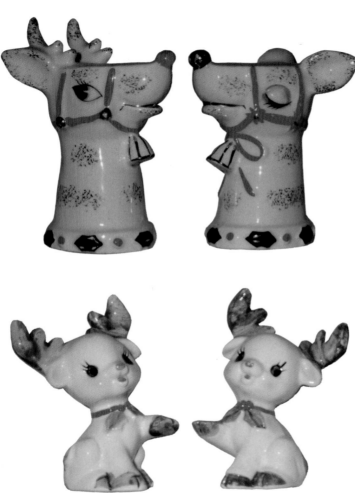

Rudolph and friend. 4". Japan. 1970s. © H.H. (Holt Howard). $25-30.

Rudolph with blue rhinestone eyes. 3.5". Japan. 1960s. Kreiss. $12-15.

Rudolph. 3". Japan. 1970s. Lefton. $12-15.

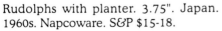
Rudolphs with planter. 3.75". Japan. 1960s. Napcoware. S&P $15-18.

Santa and Rudolph. 3". USA. 1960s. $18-20.

Santa and Rudolph nester. 3.5". Japan. 1980s. $12-15.

Rudolph and Santa in a sleigh. 3.5". Japan. 1970s. $20-25.

Rudolph in pickup truck. 4.5". China. 1994. C.I.C. $15-18.

Santa and Mrs. Claus riding Rudolphs. 4". Probably Japan. 1970s. $30-35.

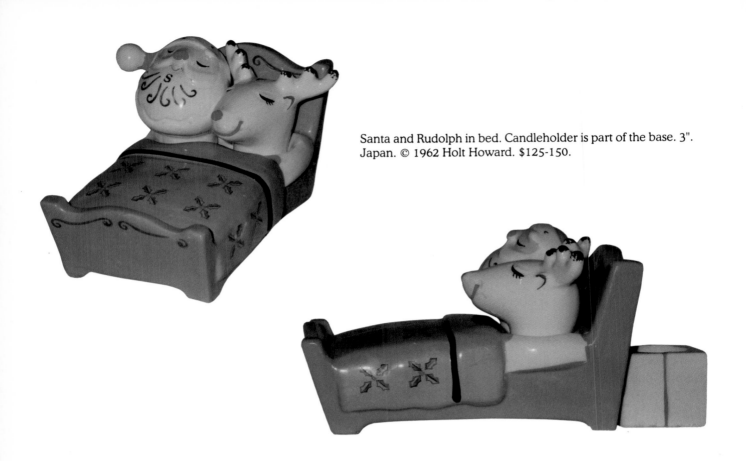

Santa and Rudolph in bed. Candleholder is part of the base. 3". Japan. © 1962 Holt Howard. $125-150.

Santa hugging Rudolph. 2.5". Plastic. Probably Hong Kong. 1960s. $5-7.

Hugging Santa/Rudolph. 3". 1978. Japan. Fitz and Floyd. $35-40.

Santa and Rudolph. 4". Taiwan. 1990s. © Robert L. May Co. Applause Inc. $18-20.

Rudolph kissing Santa. 3.75". Taiwan. 1993. Cardinal, Inc. $12-15.

Rudolph S&P with cookie jar. 4". Possibly Indonesia. Prototypes never produced by Enesco. Not priced.

Rudoph. 3". Korea. 1990s. Issued by Norcrest. $12-15.

Kermit and Miss Piggy. 5". China. 1995. Treasure Craft. © Henson. $20-25.

Kermit and Miss Piggy. 4.25". Japan. 1980s. © HA! Sigma. $125-135.

The Swedish Chef from the Muppets. 4.5". Japan. 1979. Issued by Sigma the Taste Setter. $100+.

Cookie Monster. 3.5". China. 1993. © Jim Henson Productions. Enesco. $15-20.

Elmo on fire engine. 3.75". China. 1993. © Jim Henson Productions. Enesco. $15-20.

Big Bird from Sesame Street. 4". China. 1993. © Jim Henson Productions. Enesco. $15-20.

Sad Sack from the comic strip created by George Baker while serving in the Army during WWII, and the comic book published later by Harvey Comics. 3.75". Japan. 1950s. © George Baker, Norcrest. $250.

Sharkey and Little Iodine, from "Little Iodine." 4.25". Japan © KFS, Inc., 1955 By Jimmy Hatlo. $250+.

Character chalkware sets. 2.5-3.25". USA. 1950s. $50-60 (Several sets shown have been repainted)

Blondie & Dagwood from "Blondie."

Maggie & Jiggs.

Orphan Annie and Sandy from "Little Orphan Annie."

Cap'n Midnight and Joyce from "Captain Midnight."

Barney Google & Snuffy Smith from "Barney Google."

Don Winslow and Red Pennington from "Don Winslow of The Navy."

Moon Mullins & Kayo.

Dick Tracy & Junior from "Dick Tracy."

Ziggy

Ziggy and Fuzz. 3". Japan. © Universal Press Syndicate MCMLXXIX. WWA Inc. Cleveland, USA. $40-45.

Ziggy eggs. 2.5". Taiwan. 1980s. Found in various combinations. $30-35.

Ziggy & Fuzz Christmas. 3". Japan. 1980s. © Universal Press Syndicate, MCMLXXXI, WWWA Inc., Cleveland, USA. $125-150.

ENTERTAINMENT CHARACTERS

Charlie Chaplin open salt and pepper. 3.75". Germany. 1930s.

Charlie Chaplin condiment with open salt and pepper. 5.5". Germany. 1930s. $350+.

Charlie Chaplin. 3.75". Probably USA. 1960s. $40-50.

Charlie Chaplin. 3.25". USA. 1950s. Chalkware. $85-95.

Charlie Chaplin and friend. 3.25". Czechoslovakia. 1930s. $50-60.

Charlie Chaplin and friend. 2.5". Japan. 1940s. $30-40.

Bozo the Clown. 4". Mexico. 1996. Produced by Treasure Craft for Star Jars. Unpainted clay model. $35-40.

Jerry Colonna. 5". Japan. 1960s. Suitcases are S&P. $90-100.

King Kong. 5.5". Korea. 1991. Sarsaparilla Deco Designs. $15-20.

Froggy the Gremlin condiments from "The Buster Brown Gang Show." 2.5-3". Japan. 1950s. $90-100.

The song "Frosty the Snowman" was written in 1950 and the Golden Book adapted from the song. Frosty starred in three animated TV specials in the late 1960s and 1970s. Crystal the snowgirl is Frosty's girlfriend/wife from "Frosty's Winter Wonderland."

Frosty the Snowman. 4.25". Taiwan. © Warner/Chappell Music 1990. Benjamin and Medwin Inc. $18-20.

Frosty and Crystal. 3.75". Taiwan. © Warner/Chappell Music 1991. Enesco. $20-25.

Howdy Doody in a car. 4.25". Japan. 1980s. Issued by Vandor.
$90-100.

Howdy Doody. 2.75". USA. 1950s. © Kagran. Plastic, Manufactured by Doodlings Inc., Cambridge, MA. $200+.

Clarabelle condiment. 4.25". Japan. 1950s. $175-200.

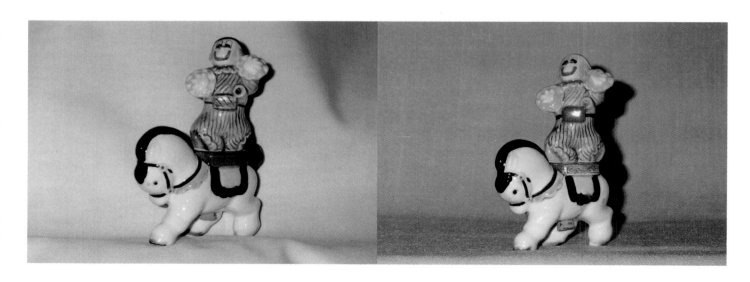

Clarabelle on a horse. 5". Japan. 1950s. $100-125.

Emmett Kelly. 3.75". Japan. 1960s. $50-60.

Emmett Kelly. 5.75". Japan. 1960. $70-80.

Emmett Kelly. 5.5". Japan. 1960s. $50-60.

Laurel & Hardy

Laurel & Hardy. 4.5". Japan. 1950s. $450+.

Laurel & Hardy. 3.5". Japan. 1950s. Incised MBS. $200+.

Laurel and Hardy. 3". USA. 1950s. Probably private ceramicist. $125-150.

Laurel & Hardy. 3.25". Japan. 1940s. $40-50.

Laurel & Hardy. 4". Germany. Dresden, 1953. $300+.

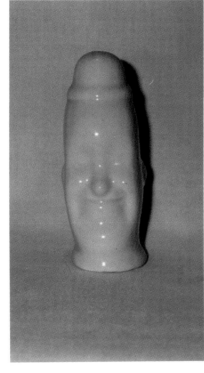

Laurel. 4". Germany. 1950s. Blue crossed swords mark. Very rare. Single, $200.

Laurel & Hardy. 4". England. 1950s. Beswick. $175+.

Laurel & Hardy. 4". Probably USA. 1960s. $150+.

Laurel and Hardy. 3". Possibly Germany. 1950s. No marks. $250+.

Dean Martin and Jerry Lewis. 3.75". Japan. 1950s. Napco. Tray says "Guess Who?" $400+.

Al Jolson and gloves. 2". USA. 1960s. Composition material, private ceramicist. $125-150.

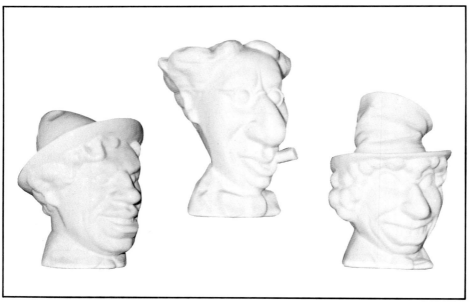

The Marx Brothers, Groucho, Zeppo, and Harpo condiment. 5". England. 1960s. $400+.

Charlie McCarthy. 2.75". Japan. 1960s. $80-90.

Charlie McCarthy. 3.25". Japan. 1950s. $50-60.

164

Nutcracker and Clara from "The Nutcracker Suite." 4.5". Taiwan. 1992. Fitz and Floyd. $25-30.

Porgy and Bess. 5.25". Copyrighted 1950, Reebs, USA. $150-175.

Dracula and Vampira. 4.5". Korea. 1992. Fitz and Floyd. $30-35.

Mario Morena, a comic from Mexico, featured in "Around the World in 80 Days." 3". Mexico. 1960s. $65-75.

Frankenstein. 3.75". Indonesia. 1990s. Enesco. $12-15.

Blackpool crest.

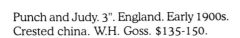

Punch and Judy. 3". England. Early 1900s.
Crested china. W.H. Goss. $135-150.

Punch & Judy. 3". 1950s. Gold lettering
Floral Bone China, England. $100-125.

Punch & Judy condiment. 3.25". Japan. 1950s. $300+.

Elvis Presley, Memphis, Tennessee. 2.5". USA. 1970s. $65-75.

The Shadow. 4.5". Probably USA. 1960s. Possibly private ceramicist. $75-85.

Yoda from Star Wars. 3.75". Japan. 1980s.
© LFL. Issued by Sigma the Taste Setter.
$200+.

R2D2 and R5D4, Droids from Star Wars. 4". Japan. 1980s. ©
LFL (Lucas Films Ltd). Issued by Sigma the Taste Setter. $200+.

Lamb Chop. 4". Taiwan. © 1993. Shari
Lewis Enterprises Inc. Benjamin and
Medwin Inc. $15-18.

From "The Wizard of Oz." 3.5". Philippines. 1990. Clay Art. $30-
35. Left: Dorothy, the Scarecrow, Cowardly Lion, and Tin Man.
Right: The Good and Wicked Witches.

MASCOTS/SYMBOLS

Loch Ness monster. 4". England. 1960s. Sylvac. $90-100.

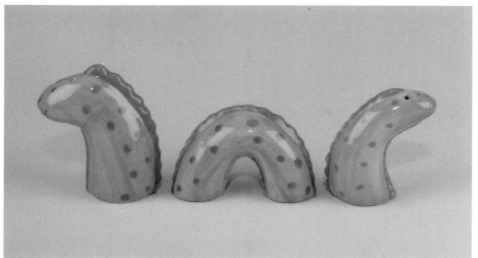

Loch Ness monster. 3". Korea. 1990s. $15-18.

Loch Ness monster. 3.25". England. 1970s. One piece set. $65-75.

Loch Ness monster. 4.25". England. 1980s. $65-75.

Mr. Kelly, the three-legged man from the Isle of Man. 2.75".
Germany. 1920s. $75-85.

Mr. Kelly condiments. Left set, 3". Right set, 3.75". Germany.
1920s. $175-200.

Jumbo. 2.5". Germany. 1930s. The name Jumbo was given to a
very large elephant by the London Zoo in the 1870s. This is the
origin of the name Jumbo for elephants. $45-50.

Smokey Bear

Smokey Bear was created by a WWII Committee of Federal officials and advertising people; Smokey first appeared in a 1945 poster. Since then, his slogan "Remember, only YOU can prevent forest fires" has become known throughout the country as the symbol of the U.S. Forest Service. Developed by Rudolph Wendelin, Smokey has appeared on posters and postage stamps and been featured in television commercials, a film, and a song.

Smokeys. 3.5". Japan. 1960s. $40-50.

Smokeys. 3.75". Japan. 1960s. $50-60.

Smokeys. 4". Japan. 1960s. $40-50.

Smokey heads. 3". Japan. 1960s. $90-100.

Smokey condiment. S&P, 3.75". Condiment, 5.25". Japan. 1960s. Norcrest. $150+.

Smokey head and hat S&P. 4.5". Mexico. 1996. Produced by Treasure Craft for Fred and Joyce Roerig, Cookie Jarrin'. $40-50.

Smokey Bear. 4.75". Japan. 1970s. $40-50.

Ranger Bear. 6". USA. 1960s. Twin Winton CA. $50-60.

Ranger Bear. 4.25". Japan. 1960s. $20-25.

Woodsy Owl. 4". Japan. 1960s. Stamped Woodsy Owl. $150+.

Kilroy. 2". USA. 1940s. Created by American troops in WWII, "Kilroy was here." $50-60.

Kilroy. 2.5". USA. 1940s. Chalkware. $25-30.

The Spuds, Mr. & Mrs. Potato Head, appeared in "Toy Story." 3.5". China. 1994. Clay Art. $18-20.

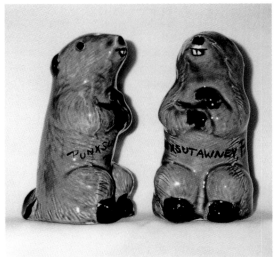

Punxatawney Phil, the groundhog weather forecaster. 4". USA. 1970s. Private ceramicist. Legend says that every year on February 2 the groundhog emerges from his hole. If it is sunny and he sees his shadow, he crawls back in his hole to sleep as there will be another six weeks of winter. If it is cloudy, winter will soon be over and he can stay awake. $25-30.

Uncle Sam. 2". USA. 1950s. Chalkware. He was a cartoon character in *The New York Lantern,* in addition to being the symbol of the USA. $35-40.

BIBLIOGRAPHY

Baumhauer, Joachim F. *Disneyana, Sammelbares aus der Welt der Micky Maus*. Battenburg Verlag, Augsburg 1993, Germany.

Cartoon Aid. Cartoon Aid Limited, London, England.

Comics and Their Creators, Life Stories of American Cartoonists. Ralph T. Hale & Company, Boston, MA, 1944.

Grant, John. *Encyclopedia of Walt Disney's Animated Characters*. Hyperion, NY.

Hake's Americana & Collectibles Auction Catalogs, York, PA.

Hake, Ted. *Hake's Guide to Comic Character Collectibles*. Wallace-Homestead Book Company, Radnor, PA.

Lotman, Jeff. *Animation Art, The Early Years 1911-1953*. Schiffer Publishing Ltd., Atglen, PA.

O'Connor, Muriel. *Muriel's Character Corner*. Novelty Salt & Pepper Shakers Club newsletter.

Sennett, Ted. *The Art of Hanna-Barbera, Fifty Years of Creativity*. Published by the Penguin Group.

The Nostalgia Collection, Pip, Squeak & Wilfred. Hawk Books Limited, London, England.

U.S. Postal Service. *American Comic Classics, A Collection of U.S. Postage Stamps*.

Zorn Karlin, Elyse. *Children Figurines of Bisque and Chinawares 1850-1950*. Schiffer Publishing Ltd., 1990.

INDEX